Leadership Lies

The Myths That Cause Leaders to Fail

By

Dave Smith

Published By

Spring Ridge Publishing

Flowery Branch, Georgia

ISBN: 9781095156735

Other Books by Dave Smith:

Growing Up Southern Style

Quips, Quotes and Funnies

Quips and Quotes, Vol 2 – Leadership

Quips and Quotes, Vol 3 – Patriots, Politicians & Pundits

Introduction

Lies! We all hear them. Sadly, we tend to believe them.

While working at WPMH Radio in Portsmouth, VA, we were reviewing sales and participating in sales training. One of the points made that day was that we needed to sell more commercial spots of a shorter length rather than longer :60 or even :30 seconds.

The recommendation was based on a recent study that stated that the more often a statement was made, the more likely the hearers were to believe the statement.

That is, the more you hear a commercial ad, the more likely you are to believe its claims.

The same is true of Leadership principles.

If you hear (or tell yourself) some Leadership concept often enough and long enough, you will begin to believe it, even if it is false.

> *The great masses of the people ... will more easily fall victims to a great lie than a small one.*
>
> *- Adolph Hitler*

Sadly, there are quite a few Leaders who may find themselves believing certain myths.

These myths inevitably lead to a downward spiral of ineffectiveness, a failure of integrity and lack success by any measurement.

In this book, we will explore some of those lies and the negative effects on the Leader and the organization.

As you read it, make a note of the LIES you have found yourself believing.

Or perhaps you see a friend or co-worker acting like the examples we've given.

You might even be asking yourself, "Why should I listen to you?"

Great question. First, may I confess that I have believed some of these lies at one point or another in my life. You might say, I know how to do it wrong.

In the pages that follow, we don't profess to say that we've never succumbed to the failures described here. Just the opposite is more truthful.

But then, the truth is the truth. Even the ancient prophets warned that men and women would tend to believe a lie rather than the truth.

As you read these pages, I hope you will make a list of the lies you have found yourself believing and start the hard work of telling yourself the truth.

You can break the patterns of behavior based on believing these lies!

For

Kenny & Janet,

Two of the reasons I want to be a better Leader

THE LIES

1. "My Job Is to Give Orders"
2. "You Can Only Trust Yourself"
3. "I'm the Leader Because "I'm Smarter"
4. "Money Is Enough"
5. "I Don't Have Time to Socialize"
6. "They Can Like It or Lump It"
7. "People are the problem"
8. "Everybody Loves Me"
9. "I Just Need to Talk the Talk"
10. "Evaluations Aren't Important"
11. "I'm Indispensable!"
12. "It's Better to Not Make Hard Decisions"
13. "Whatever Happened Before Isn't Important"
14. "It's Not My Fault"
15. "I Have to Watch Everyone"
16. "That's Not Important"

Epilogue

Selected Resources

#1

"My Job Is to Give Orders"

This is the traditional view of Leadership. But it is a lie. Previous generations of Leaders operated based on this assumption and it could be said that there was some level of success.

That method of Leadership succeeded because both the Leader and the follower expected this kind of behavior.

It's not our job here to evaluate whether this approach was correct, but in its historical context, it certainly could be considered to have been effective.

Today, we have discovered that Leadership is more effective when team members "buy in" to the direction the Leader wishes to go.

> *"If your actions inspire others to dream more, learn more, do more, and become more, you are a Leader."*
>
> *- John Quincy Adams*

Later we will talk about the not being fearful in decision-making, but for now we need to realize that an organization is most successful when Leaders are not required nor choose to make all decisions.

Empowering team members to make appropriately delegated decisions makes an organization and an individual Leader more efficient and effective.

Every new Leader wants to change something.

In fact, if a change were not needed, there may not be a need for you at all.

The temptation is to move right in, announce some new marching orders and try to establish yourself as the "top dog."

You will find that taking this approach promotes fear and creates instability in your team. Your team members are more highly motivated by the fear of loss than the anticipation of gain.

The fact is, Leadership is a paradox.

On the one hand, some believe that Leadership is all about being "in charge," strong and forceful.

Yet, many of the most successful Leaders are those who can harness the power of "synergy."

You might ask, "Yes, but don't you run the risk of being taken advantage of – of others climbing the success ladder over you?"

Yes, Leadership is risky business. It is not for the faint of heart!

But, taking the "I'm the Boss; I make the decisions around here" approach is ineffective and out of date. Acting in concert with this lie can cause Leaders to get caught up in their own world as if it is "all about me."

The usual sequence is that Leaders begin to be so busy with making all the decisions that there is little time for anything else.

Workload spirals upward for this Leader further isolating her from the team.

As a result, a self-fulfilling prophecy of "I give the orders and make all the decisions" begins to develop. The Leader's own workload increases to the point that they *can't* know the skills of the team members, so delegation becomes non-existent.

> *Half the harm that is done in this world is due to people who want to feel important.*
>
> *- T.S. Eliot*

When delegation is thought to be impossible, the "I Give Orders" Leader is forced to take on more tasks and the cycle repeats itself.

Forgotten is the truth that when you make the transition from a "do-er" to a Leader, your responsibilities change significantly.

Sadly, many Leaders are more infatuated with the idea of being called the "Boss" than actually learning to lead.

They seem to see themselves in the role of the one who has the answer to every question to prove how much they know.

For some who believe this lie, the most important issue is the pay scale, the job title and getting their name on the top of the org chart.

This attitude also reveals more about the fears and inability to trust subordinates than any exceptional decision-making ability of the Leader.

This kind of fear might be based on a prior bad experience. If that's the case, take an honest look at what happened.

Ask yourself:

- Did you fully train the employee?
- Did you outline the parameters the team member was to follow in making the decision?
- Did you coach the employee after the incident?

If the answer to these questions is "yes," then it's time to move on.

If the pattern persists with other team members, then examine your methods and style of communicating. The message may not be getting across.

If you have individual employees who persist in making poor work decisions, then personal attention is needed. This might range from retraining to removing from the role.

Then too, some believe this lie because it's the easiest way to operate.

We tend to think it takes less effort to just "give orders" rather than train trustworthy and talented staff members, delegate authority and follow-up.

But problems come because when the Leader makes all the decisions, she must *continue* to make all the decisions.

Initially it may take more effort to hire well, train effectively and follow-up wisely. But that effort is "front-loaded." In the long run, acting contrary to the "just give orders" lie is the real time saver.

For some individuals in Leadership positions, believing this lie comes easily because we want to dominate others. This desire is often based in a sense of entitlement.

When one feels entitled, the opinions or efforts of others matters not at all. All that does matter is what I think, feel or do.

As will often happen in the coming pages, this is a good moment to ask yourself a few questions.

- How well do you understand your personality type?
- Is there a pattern in your typical style in personal interactions?
- Do you tend to be active or passive?
- Do you prefer to be "in charge" or are you comfortable serving under competent Leaders?

If you haven't done so, find one of the easy to understand personality profiles and take an honest self-evaluation.

I prefer the ones with four categories like the DISC™ profile because it is readily available and doesn't require specialized training to understand.

If you tend to act as if you believe this lie, it may be because it is your personal, natural way to act, based on your personality type.

But don't blame your poor management and Leadership methods on a "that's just the way I am" excuse.

Instead, take a proactive, cognizant approach to your Leadership style. Leadership is not just what seems easy or convenient. Don't focus on what seems to be a quick fix by just barking out orders.

Your job is not to just give orders. Your job is to *Lead*. The best approach to leading a team is based on truth, not based on prior bad experiences or an easy, personality-default style.

Always remember that the relational equity you build by engaging your team is more powerful than your positional authority.

#2

"You Can Only Trust Yourself"

This lie is related to most of the other Lies we'll discuss but deserves its own treatment because of the widespread impact it has.

The lack of trust for team members and employees will surely poison your Leadership effectiveness. If you don't trust others, you cannot delegate, you cannot inspire, you cannot provide objective feedback – you cannot Lead!

Instead, you'll tend to sabotage your organization and its future Leaders.

Trust is a critical factor in giving significant responsibility to team members who have some level of Leadership potential. Leaders who believe this lie tend to delegate only small or "token" responsibilities rather than significant or "real" responsibility.

> *"Self-Trust is the first secret to success."*
>
> *- Ralph Waldo Emerson*

This "fake" kind of delegation helps the deceived Leader believe that he or she is developing future Leaders when just the opposite is true.

It's just another way of putting up-and-coming Leaders in a box from where they will never escape.

The tendency to believe this lie is often based in fear, low self-esteem, change resistance or an emotional connection to their job.

You might be surprised that "fear" is in this list of justifications for believing this lie.

This kind of deceived Leader often compensates for this fear by showing emotional distance from employees (see "I Don't Have Time to Socialize") or by an over-the-top arrogance.

Also, low self-esteem can contribute to the mis-belief that "You Can Only Trust Yourself."

It takes a healthy self-image to trust others. Giving up some level of authority or power requires a degree of confidence that, even if "things go badly," one can recover from any negative consequences.

In other words, a Leader must learn to trust themselves before they can trust others.

Some Leaders believe this lie because they are simply unwilling to change. They don't see a need to trust others because, in their minds, "Everything is working just fine. Why mess it up by changing things?"

This unwillingness to change is related to the fear we discussed – the fear of an unpredictable outcome.

One Leader I encountered had been the "assistant" for several years before assuming the main Leadership role in the organization. What we quickly discovered was that "nothing" was going to significantly change.

This new Leader was stereotypically a "manager." He saw his role as maintaining the status quo.

Rather than being the Leader who thought it was his job to "Give Orders," he failed to trust anyone because that might bring change.

The goal of preserving the status quo became even clearer when every subsequent promotion went to the "heir apparent" of whatever job was vacant.

The fear that allows this mis-belief can also be based on the fear of being replaced.

After all, if your "underlings" are never able to show their "stuff", then they can never take your place!

In some ways the current job and its processes bring a kind of emotional stability to some Leaders. This emotional aspect cannot be overlooked.

For some, the emotional bond to a lack of trust is the issue of job security itself. They seem to ask, "What would I do," and "Where would I go?"

Another self-protective mechanism is the thought that, "If you don't trust anyone, no one can disappoint you, right?"

This Leader also seems to say, "If you don't trust anyone, no one can take your job away because they find out about some fault or shortcoming you have, right?

What gets lost are the achievements your team can make by trusting – delegating, inspiring and providing objective feedback to them. Remember, when your team achieves – who gets the credit first – YOU do!

By not allowing your team to reach its highest potential, your organization and YOU lose.

For some, another aspect of fear and the emotional connection to a job is fear of retirement.

When one's self-worth comes from work over a long period of time, then the potential loss of self-worth that could come from retirement is a genuine fear.

In one office of a large organization, the company had a healthy retirement program that could pay the retiree nearly as much as their salary after a designated number of years.

An individual I knew had worked several years beyond the required number of years to retire with full benefits.

Each subsequent year of work had no effect on this individual's retirement benefit due to a cap on the benefit.

Friend after friend demonstrated to her that she was mathematically losing money by continuing to work.

Her retirement pay would have netted her more than her regular paycheck. It became clear that financial benefit had no impact on her thinking.

Her reason for staying on at work was simply that she didn't know what she would do with her time if she did retire.

Every individual must figure out for themselves what justification they use as the basis for their lack of trust in others.

Whether it is a previous bad experience, a fear of change in general or some unknown fear of the future, great Leaders find a way around these obstacles.

Work to become an intellectually and emotionally healthy Leader. Be honest with yourself.

Be the Leader you were meant to be!

#3

"I'm the Leader Because I'm Smarter"

Most of us have worked with a "know it all." This Leader is under the misconception that a high level of education or experience makes them superior to others.

In some situations, it's a case where "inside information" is used as a tool to dominate other team members.

Leaders who believe this lie often have an inflated sense of self-worth and personal pride.

In this case, it's not only "all about me" but it's about my education, expertise and my desire to show it to others.

Maybe it's the long-term employee who helped develop a "special procedure" or process.

I recall just such a Leader whose first approach to other employees was to use his deep voice and tall stature to intimidate them.

He was the resident expert on some special processes and in fact, had written much of the employee manual for those processes.

On one occasion, our team needed to take some of those special steps and it was vitally important for every detail to be correct.

I sent one of our team members to this Leader's office to get some instruction and to verify that we were following the steps precisely.

As usual, this Leader acted in his "normal" way and berated her for not already knowing the correct details.

When she returned, she came directly to my office and stated bluntly, "If you ever send me to his office again, I'll quit before I go back!"

Perhaps it's the Leader with the law degree or special certification who feels compelled to put every word of a memo, document or decision under a microscope.

You know her.

Every meeting becomes a discussion of the microscopic meaning of words or punctuation. The ancient Hebrews called these the "jots and tittles" of Biblical meanings.

This Leader can often be heard saying, "Here, let me do it."

Or they may say, "You just don't understand."

> *"Knowing yourself is the beginning of wisdom."*
>
> *-Aristotle*

What this kind of Leader doesn't understand is that there is something more important than knowledge or intelligence.

And perhaps we've brought it on ourselves as an untended consequence of focusing on training and education.

What this Leader misunderstands is the need for "Wisdom."

It's not considered often enough.

You might call it by other terms like insight, perception or judgement. It's one of those characteristics that is difficult to objectively quantify but we recognize it when we see it. And, we recognize when it is absent as well.

The Oxford Dictionary defines wisdom as the act of "having or showing experience, knowledge, and good judgement."

Another plain English definition I've heard is "knowing how life works."

Ancient King Solomon has been heralded as the "wisest man on earth." He wrote that "the fear and reverence of God is the beginning of wisdom" (Proverbs 9:10). The New Testament says that wisdom is available to all who will simply ask for it.

Ancient Israel's religious law, prophecy, and approach to wisdom were not exclusive to Israel but were shared by other ancient Near Eastern cultures. Wisdom was an exalted way of thinking in that part of the ancient world. This wisdom described a way of viewing and approaching life and involved instructing the young in practical and personal conduct and answering philosophical questions about life's meaning.

> *"Experience is not what happens to you; it is what you do with what happens to you."*
> *- Aldous Huxley*

Whether one is a Christian Believer or not, it makes perfect sense that wisdom comes from the recognition that information alone is not enough to make the best Leadership decisions.

It comes from a combination of experience tempered with understanding the "smart" choices made by those who have gone before.

We equate wisdom with age, but age itself is no guarantee. Age only reflects the number of opportunities one may have had to learn how life works.

The question is, will you learn from life experiences, from those who have demonstrated wisdom before you and learn how to properly *apply* the information you've absorbed?

The criterion for great Leadership has nothing to do with intelligence.

What does matter in Leadership is personal growth. Information without the accompanying tool of application is just an encyclopedia.

John Maxwell in his book, "Developing The Leader Within You," describes three phases of the growth process.

First, one must Learn. This is the information gathering step. It comes from intentional observation, reading and listening. The second phase is that one must UNLearn. This is the step where you find that some of your assumptions are false – that you have, perhaps inadvertently, believed one of these lies.

It may be that Leaders you have observed seemed to be correct and successful. However, over time, your own experience and with the benefit of perspective, you find they were wrong.

This is harder than the Learn step, but it is just as important.

Then, you will need to RE-Learn. This is the stage of growth where you refine what you have learned and make updated and improved decisions.

If you are not un-learning and relearning, you are not really learning!

Don't get caught up in believing you are a Leader because you are the "smartest."

#4

"Money Is Enough"

"A decent wage is enough," I heard one Leader say. "I don't need to 'baby' them with praise and compliments. Besides, what do I do then when they make a mistake – take it all back?"

This Leader is lying to himself if he believes the only motivation for employees or subordinates is money. Far from it.

According to the website www.accessperks.com, reporting a Robert Half survey, less than half of all employees would leave for another job just for more money.

> *Your job is to hire enthusiastic people and then not make them unenthusiastic."*
>
> *– Philip Crosby*

In fact, 58% of workers say they'd start a job with a lower salary if that meant working for a great boss (Randstad).

Also, the Muse (www.themuse.com) reports that 89% of employers think workers leave for more money when only 12% actually do. Around 75% of people voluntarily leaving jobs "quit their boss, not their job."

So why do Leaders think money is enough?

Sadly, the answer seems to be simply an unwillingness to engage the actual performance of a team member.

The justification that praise puts the Leader in an untenable position when correction is needed is just a red herring. It's a matter of giving praise *correctly* and *timely*.

> *"I've yet to find the man, however exalted his station, who did not do better work and put forth the greater effort under a spirit of approval than under a spirit of criticism."*
>
> - Charles Schwab

Here are some tips for giving appropriate, positive feedback. It is adapted from a list developed by www.employeeconnect.com.

First – be direct. When our expectations are met, we tend to assume that the person is already aware and ignore giving appreciation. That's not necessarily the case.

Then, be specific.

This is not the time to say, "I like your work. You are a great guy." Instead, give examples and avoid baseless sentiment.

Remember also to give feedback timely, whether it is a compliment or correction. The closer to the event you give feedback, the more the employee connects their behavior to your feedback.

Next, choose the right place for feedback. Offering positive feedback in public can be helpful, especially if giving kudos to a group.

However, negative feedback should always be in private.

If you must give positive and negative feedback, sandwich the negative between positive items if possible.

And, remember, your way of doing it is usually not the only way or perhaps not even the best way.

The staffing agency, Robert Half, gives these pointers on giving negative employee feedback:

- **Strike a professional tone**
    - Check your temper and wait until you're calm.
- **Emphasize facts not feelings**
    - Address the problem, not your frustrations.
    - Offer some specific suggestions.

- **Watch your words**
  - Avoid demoralizing statements that question the employee's intelligence.
  - Avoid subjective statements. ("You're not showing enough drive lately") and sweeping generalizations ("You never contribute ideas during brainstorming sessions").
- **Be direct when giving feedback**
  - Avoidance deprives employees of information they could use to improve.
  - Aim to be kind but candid.
- **Be clear when giving feedback:**
  - "I'm concerned your chronic tardiness is starting to hurt your performance and reputation."

- **Make it a two-way conversation** o Keep an open mind.
    - o Give team members an opportunity to explain their side of the story.
    - o You may discover a problem that is a symptom of a larger underlying issue.
- **Focus on the fix**
    - o You have one end goal: to make sure that the issue is swiftly rectified
- **Balance negative feedback with praise**

Don't be the Leader who comments only when employees slip up. Consistently offer kudos when it's warranted.

Not knowing how or when to communicate praise to team members isn't the issue.

It is simply an issue of "Are you willing to take the time to do it?"

When you take the time to recognize achievements of your team, the results are improved morale and higher achievement.

It's not just about company picnics and "goodies" at work. Team members do appreciate those perks. But effective engagement with your team is more than hot dogs and snacks.

Team members want to know that Leaders care about their work, their co-workers and the organization.

Money is NOT enough. Your team wants and deserves more.

#5

"I Don't Have Time to Socialize"

Usually this lie is accompanied by the sub-lie, "I'm too busy for that. I have important work to do!"

Or another red herring, "Besides, you can't be friends with anyone at work."

Believers in this lie are often guilty of believing the lie we've just discussed, that "Money Is Enough."

In a more general sense when you believe both of these lies, you are failing to sufficiently interact with your team and positively motivate them.

Too often these Leaders refuse to believe that engaging with employees does affect the bottom line.

Aloofness, according to Jay C. Rifenbary in his book, "True To Your Core" (p67) is nothing more than "misguided self-confidence."

When you say you don't have "time," you are really saying that you are too important to be bothered with other people who are, by definition, less important than you.

Be respectful of people. Remember that they notice how you behave and when you interact with them.

A Leader in one large organization was faced with the task of handling a layoff.

His role was to inform those who would remain that others were being released. That would seem to be the "better" role to be assigned, right?

> *The happiest people are those who have invested their time in others.*
>
> *- John Maxwell*

Sadly, this Leader discovered that his very presence in the work area created a suspicion that "something was up."

He quickly realized, although his normal work duties rarely demanded interaction with this particular group, that he needed to show up when "nothing" was up!

This Leader's behavior was not motivated by any sense of aloofness or lack of desire to interact with the Team, but the normal flow of work simply didn't require regular interaction.

If you are relatively new in a position of Leadership, you may not realize it or think that the attention is deserved, but your team does notice what you do.

We will repeat the theme over and over again. People are relational. Don't overlook the human side of the work equation.

You have a nice office and your own slate of work to accomplish. Your team is "out there" disconnected and disengaged from you.

It's hard to lead anyone who doesn't know who you are, your Leadership style, or if you are even interested in them.

In one supervisory training session I attended, the primary facilitator made recommendations that tended to further isolate the Leader from team members.

His rather odd suggestions included:

- Removing the chairs from your office (to keep your employees from "dropping in" to talk)
- Standing when someone enters your office (to make them hurry up and leave) and,
- Keeping a stack of "busy work" to hand out to employees who seemed to have nothing better to do than drop in.

These were all predicated on the "I'm Too Busy" lie. Don't do it!

Instead, get out of your office every day. Make sure your team sees you.

Let your staff know that a closed door means only urgent interruptions and an open door means just that.

You may have heard of a management style called, "Management By Walking Around." Although this technique came to be popular in the 1970's, it is based on President Lincoln's informal "inspections" of the Union Army during the Civil War.

Venture out to get a sense of the workplace. Take a minute to stop and briefly chat with your team members. You'll learn some things.

For example, during a time when I was on a user testing team for a new software system, our CEO dropped by a retirement reception I was attending. He moved around and said hello to the retiring employee and others.

We were acquainted but I didn't have regular contact with the CEO. Knowing I was on a special assignment for the testing, he asked how it was going.

I tried to avoid getting into the multiple problems we were facing.

Sensing I was beating around the bush, he asked more directly, "So, Dave, would you say the new system is user friendly?"

I looked at my fellow tester nearby, then caught the eye of my boss who seemed to say, "Tell him the truth."

My reply was, "No sir. We have found it is not user friendly at all. It is very difficult to navigate for the areas we use."

Late that afternoon, the CEO sent for my boss, my fellow system tester and me. With more detailed questions answered, the CEO stated that he would "have a talk" with the head of the system development team to see what could be done to make life easier for users.

Without his brief appearance at the reception, we may have had even further delays and problems with the new system.

Ultimately, the system was reconfigured in a way to make the system easier to use.

Your team will notice when you "socialize" with them. It tells them you care about them.

It may not reflect reality, but when your employees see you socializing with others but not them, they automatically assume that they have a lower stature.

Your goal as a Leader is to raise the level of your team's self-image. When your team believes that they are an important part of the overall work of the organization, their performance is very likely to improve.

That truthful belief comes from you.

In another section of this book we will discuss the Leadership tool of Accountability. But, when you make a point of interacting positively with your team, you take advantage of another tool - Inspiration.

Don't overlook this tool! As team members get to know you as the positive, optimistic, likeable, consistent Leader you are becoming, Inspiration will start to work for you.

The intangible benefits of "Inspiration" can't be overstated.

Employees will move from "whatever" to "whatever it takes" when they feel a sense of camaraderie with each other and loyalty to you.

No amount of money, pressure, brow-beating or cajoling is as effective as Inspiration.

When you've done your homework with your team and its individuals, you improve your ability to make smart judgements. The added interaction will fuel your knowledge base of your team and the issues you face.

MAKE time to interact with your team!

#6

"They Can Like It or Lump It"

In one organization I know, this was practically a quote from a high-ranking manager in the group. The paraphrase usually went like this: "If they don't like what I tell them to do, they can just quit. I'll get someone who'll do just as much work for less money!"

Sadly, there are many Leaders who believe this lie. Most don't dare vocalize it.

Still, it's reflected in a kind of disdain for employees and at least a touch of arrogance.

While in a position which required reviewing actions such as hiring and promoting, I had a surprising encounter with this kind of attitude.

A manager who had followed the process for hiring, selected a candidate and forwarded the paperwork to me for my review.

After my detailed review, I forwarded the final documents to my manager who usually just signed the selection approval documents and returned them to me.

Typically, even if he felt the selected individual was not the absolute best fit for the job, he usually took the attitude of, "Well, you'll be the one to have to directly deal with the new hire, not me."

This time, he called me to his office for a closed-door meeting for the first time in over 100 hiring/promotion transactions.

He simply returned the documents to me and instructed me to tell the hiring manager to, "pick someone else" and gave no reasons.

I later discovered that my boss and the selected individual were from the same small town and that my boss considered the individual to be of a lower class than he.

It was a classic case of disdain for a person with no basis in the work ability or characteristics of the individual.

This mis-belief also demonstrates a theme we repeat from time to time, "If you have to do or say something to prove you are the boss, the head-honcho, the big cheese…then you ain't!"

Let's make an admission right here. There will be times when your decisions won't be popular. If you regularly communicate with your staff, you will know when it is the case.

> *People constantly underestimate their abilities and it is the responsibility of parents, coaches and teachers [Leaders] to raise their self-image and expectations.*
>
> *- Football Coach Lou Holtz*

What you can do and should be doing is mitigating the impact of unpopular decisions. When you can, explain the facts behind the decision. When you can't, take the high road, and be considerate of your team members.

If the decision is a cutback or layoff, give those affected an opportunity to vent to you in private (since you would have delivered the news in private). Make it clear that you understand the impact that the decision has on them.

The "Like It or Lump It" lie that Leaders believe reveals that they hold their employees in low esteem. It bears repeating that you cannot succeed without a great team.

Thinking that you can just replace team members is shortsighted and fails to take into account several factors.

First, this kind of management attitude encourages a high turnover rate. Turnover is expensive!

There is usually a gap of time between when one employee leaves an another takes their place.

Here's the question, "Who is doing the work of the lost employee during the interim?" Right, nobody.

Then, how long will it take the new employee to be sufficiently trained to produce as well as the former employee? Would it be a week, a month, three months or even more?

Every day it takes to get the team operating at full capacity is productivity lost *forever*!

If you have team members who can be salvaged or coached into higher performance, it will be worth the effort.

We have said and will repeat just how important it is for you to interact and accurately evaluate your staff. You can only do that if you get to know them.

Yes, there will be situations where someone is in the wrong position. They may be doomed to failure.

Do you know where their skills would be best suited? Were they effectively trained for their current position?

If they can't be salvaged, you may need to release them. Still, most organizations as well as common sense requires that you document efforts to retrain the employee and given them time to respond.

The term we use now for personnel departments is "Human Resources." That term may seem a bit impersonal, but it accurately reflects your best tool for accomplishing your business goals – PEOPLE. Don't take them for granted!

Believing this lie will cost you and company productivity.

Don't fall for it!

#7

"People are the Problem"

It is a lie to think that the people who work around you are the problem. It's not the fault of that "incompetent" manager above you or that troublesome employee who answers to you.

Oh, that's not to say that others don't have problems or even cause them.

Some Leaders even tell themselves this lie: "My job would be so much easier if it weren't for my staff." The truth is, without your staff, you would have no job!

The issue for Leaders is that managing your staff is not your "problem," it is your primary job responsibility!

Once you become a Leader, remember that the emphasis should shift from "doing" to "leading."

Leadership is both a noun and a verb. For too long, too many of us have considered Leadership to be only a state of being based on position or status or title. But Leadership is the act of leading. It is the very function of leading.

It is not passive. It is active, engaged and involved.

Sadly, in many organizations, managers have a custom of promoting to Leadership only those who were highly competent at their old position.

Most of us are familiar with what has been dubbed, "The Peter Principle." Now the term even has a dictionary entry in Merriam-Webster!

We've backed ourselves into an organizational corner by believing that success in one job prepares an individual for another role.

> *"In a hierarchy every employee tends to rise to his level of incompetence... [I]n time every post tends to be occupied by an employee who is incompetent to carry out its duties... Work is accomplished by those employees who have not yet reached their level of incompetence."*
>
> *-Laurence J. Peter*

In fact, it may or may not.

When was the last time you saw a vacancy announcement that did NOT ask for a certain period of time in a role subordinate to the vacant position.

We need to re-think the relationship between job knowledge or success in a journeyman role and the requirements for leading that group or some other group of journeyman level employees

Organizations also unwittingly follow the "Peter Principle" by promoting incompetent managers to levels where it was though they could "do the least damage."

In one organization, a Leader had become ineffective due to his micromanaging of his team (See the chapters "I Have to Watch Everyone!" and "I'm Indispensable.")

His management team was aware of the problem but were unwilling or unable to take drastic measures such as suspension or firing.

Instead, this Leader was reassigned to manage a team which had historically operated very independently. This new group generated their own "prospects", had extremely low turnover, functioned mostly out of the office and was very productive.

Unfortunately, this Leader's behavior cut the production in half and developed discord that had never existed in the group.

This Leader had been effective when left to himself to work. "Leadership" was not in his skill set.

Eventually he was assigned duties that did not involve leading others.

When people seem to be in the middle of problems, it is the Leaders job to step in.

Move it, change it, retool it or shake it up some other way. Put the right people in the right jobs.

To put it bluntly, your staff is not the problem, YOU are.

A Leader who fails to make the shift from "do-er" to manager is bound for failure. In the same way you became skilled at your "do-er" job, learn the skills necessary to "manage" the job.

Here are some ideas:

First, quit blaming someone else and take responsibility for your team. There are few in your organization who are in a better position to improve the performance of your team. (We'll talk more about "blame" later.)

You know, or should know, the strengths and weaknesses of your team members.

You know, or should know, your *own* strengths and weaknesses.

Use that information to make the needed changes. Proactively work to improve your own personal development. Read books. Listen to audio.

If you don't know the name John Maxwell, you have been living in a Leadership vacuum. He was recently recognized as the foremost expert on Leadership in the 21st Century in the world!

You should have a shelf full of Leadership books and be reading one continually.

Leaders *can* be made!

When you take these steps, you will be able to identify your real superstars. Those are the ones you should promote.

Then, be sure to learn how to manage conflict effectively.

Unresolved conflict becomes the "elephant in the room" any time differing individuals meet.

It's up to you to detect tension, negative emotions and polarization and diffuse this ticking time bomb. People are only a problem when you hire, promote or delegate unwisely.

No one like to be thought of as simply a small cog in a big machine. To be a Leader and not just a manager, you need to focus on people as people.

People are your business.

#8

"Everybody Loves Me"

This lie could be stated, "I can get away with anything because I'm loved. I can charm my way out of anything."

Leaders with personal charisma often tell themselves this lie. This may be the most dangerous lie of all we'll discuss. At its root is a self-deception and very often reveals character flaws in a dramatic way.

The Leaders who tell themselves this lie often have achieved position after position with their charming and gregarious nature. We all want to be around pleasant individuals, right?

> *Character is what you are in the dark.*
>
> *- D.L. Moody*

When this individual reaches a Leadership level, they far too often deceive themselves into believing that charm is all it takes and that they are really "special."

I have bad news. It ain't so.

This kind of super-ego is often inadvertently perpetuated. These Leaders tend to surround themselves with adoring supporters who are anxious to please and initially will overlook either incompetence or unwise decision-making.

In the process, the Leader gets poor advice or no advice at all because of a fear of offending him. The goal of the Leader is adoration and he gets it because adoration and loyalty is what gets rewarded.

The truth is that every human on earth wants appreciation, respect and yes, even love from those around them. When the workplace becomes the incubator for these emotions, the Leader, team members and organization are all at risk.

Trouble is on the horizon.

Just a cursory recollection of recent history shows us that self-deception affects Leaders from Presidents to Preachers and everyone in between.

One could debate the wisdom of the impeachment proceedings involving President Bill Clinton on and on. The charges were lying to a Grand Jury and resulting alleged obstruction of justice. President Clinton's defenders have been known to say, "It was just sex."

May I suggest that the entire "mess" actually had its basis in the lie that "Everyone Loves Me" and therefore I can do what I want.

There is additional evidence that some women were paid out of court settlements in exchange for their silence as well. *https://www.businessinsider.com/these-are-the-sexualassault-allegations-against-bill-clinton-2017-11*

Each person must determine the voracity of the accusations for themselves. However, it is not beyond reason to believe that this kind of behavior could be the result of this self-deception.

Many remember the scandal that surrounded Rev. Jim Bakker. His fall was a result of "hush money paid to a church secretary, Jessica Hahn, for alleged rape."

Subsequent investigation led to his indictment on financial fraud charges and resulted in conviction, imprisonment and divorce. *https://en.wikipedia.org/wiki/Jim_Bakker*

Interestingly, in his book entitled, "I Was Wrong" Bakker confessed that, though he was personally responsible for his behavior and decisions, he had surrounded himself with followers who wouldn't say "no" to his whims.

One could speculate that those followers had their own selfish motives in giving in to what they perceived as Bakker's desires.

However, by his own words, the admitted fault was ultimately with Mr. Bakker and no one else. *http://www.spiritwatch.org/firejbwrong.htm*

Clearly, he believed that "Everyone" loved him.

If you see yourself in these pages, start now to separate yourself from this lie. Consider that first, "everybody" does not love you – and that is o.k.

The truth is that many of those who seem to be your adoring fans, primarily have their own interests in mind.

They have discovered that you reward loyalty and "affection" with pay raises and promotions.

Let's say that there are those around you who genuinely appreciate you. That still does not give you license to behave any way you want. Your behavior will be scrutinized by those above you. You will be discovered.

Some of your behavior may be grounds for your dismissal. Besides – it may be illegal!

Often at the root of the kind of thinking that accepts this kind of lie is the absence of a "Leaders heart." Heart.

It's a word not often associated with Leadership but is as intertwined as the nerve endings in the human body. It is the pathway for the signals that come from the ego to the brain.

Those signals seem to originate from a mysterious part of the human being.

There is somehow, somewhere, a large part of us that wants our own way.

When those signals overpower the signals that go from the heart to the brain, we are headed for trouble.

You can call it ego or use whatever terminology you choose. Still, the desire to live without rules, restrictions or a code of conduct is self-destructive.

Leadership can't be truly and fully successful without a "heart" for the team members around you and for the organization.

When the team and the organization become

> *"Leadership is a potent combination of strategy and character. But, if you must be without one, be without the strategy."*
>
> *-Gen. Norman Schwarzkopf*

more important than our need for attention or affection, we can exhibit the strongest traits of a Leader.

Back at F.T. Wills High School in Smyrna, Georgia, our football team had become known for playing for the other team's Homecoming Games. (You always wanted to schedule someone you could beat, right?)

In the second year of my participation in the program, the coach of our highly successful basketball team was recruited to be an assistant football coach.

The fact that Coach Blankenship had previously neither played nor coached football didn't matter.

What did seem to matter was that Coach Blankenship talked over and over about having "heart." As a 16 year-old junior backup lineman, I heard him preach that my evident lack of physical skills could be overcome with heart.

We learned that it is always too early to quit.

We learned that the player who put the team and the school's reputation first could somehow find something within him to muster up extra strength when there seemed to be none before.

> *"I have nothing to offer but blood, toil, tears and sweat."*
>
> *-Winston Churchill*

The Leader who focuses on his own small popularity and cravings for attention has surrendered his heart to his ego instead of his team.

In Christianity, this inward struggle is called a battle between the "flesh" and the "spirit." Whatever terminology you use, don't lose this most important battle!

It may seem that "Everyone Loves" you. This lie is a trap to be avoided at all costs!

#9

"I Just Need To Talk The Talk"

This lie often takes the form of "As long as I talk the talk, it doesn't matter what I actually do."

Closely related to "They Love Me," this lie reveals a basic misunderstanding (or self-deception) that it's more important to look or "sound" good than to produce results.

Another characteristic of the charismatic Leader is that he or she has learned the "lingo" but refuses or is unable to lead beyond the surface. Public image is more important than productivity.

With this self-told lie, the Leader has likely seen positive effects of talking the talk and fallen for the deception.

It's important to point out that verbal inspiration is, in fact a part of Leadership. Never overlook the power of your words and the attitudes they reflect.

Not just, "Rah, Rah, Let's Go Get 'Em," talk, an effective Leader learns to wisely (there's that word again) communicate goals, vision and plans.

It is true that Leaders do not need to communicate every bit of information at their disposal. There are often high-level discussions leading to a policy or decision that can't be shared, of course.

But giving frequent, positive words from the Leader pays big dividends.

The issue is that "words" must be followed up with corresponding, consistent actions.

> *"Those who know, don't talk. Those who talk, don't know.*
>
> *- Lao Tzu*

Speaking without acting is often the result of two self-defeating thought processes.

The first is that words don't need to be followed by actions. The second is that the Leader may feel *unable* to effectively act.

Failing to act consistently with your words is often a simple failure of integrity.

Take a look inside. Does the truth matter to you? I'm not referring to withholding confidential information, but rather, purposeful deception.

> *"People do what people see."*
>
> *-Unknown*

There are multiple measures of integrity, but one of them is to do what you say you'll do.

I served in one organization where I shared an office space with my manager. My predecessor had produced a sign which the manager posted on the wall behind his desk.

It read, "DWYSYWD" – Do What You Said You Said You Would Do.

I couldn't look toward his desk without being confronted with that truth. Admittedly, it had a profound impact on me.

I've not been perfect in obeying that admonition, but now, many years later, I still cannot ignore its message.

It is more difficult to overcome the "Talk Only" lie when the Leader isn't convinced that consistent action is vital.

Believing this lie is often the result of being able to "skate by" with just talk for a long period of time. Too often, this Leader has convinced himself that actions don't have to match words. Worse yet, they sometimes believe that their actions actually do match their words.

More bad news – it ain't so.

However, there is hope for Leaders who somehow don't believe they have the ability to act!

There's an old question that asks, "Are Leaders born or made?"

The correct answer is, "Yes."

There are some individuals who seem to have an innate ability to lead. The rest of us must learn to lead.

Fortunately, Leaders can be transformed with the right training.

There is an encyclopedia of resources for the Leaders. Next to "self-help" books, Leadership books are everywhere. Effective Leaders are almost always readers.

Certainly, the best Leaders look to sources around them to improve their skills.

Whether it's a co-worker, "unofficial" mentors, seminars or books, certain skills need updating just like modern computer programmers need to learn the latest software.

For those of you in non-Leadership roles, start the preparation now. If you are, or are becoming a great journeyman employee, a great "worker bee," at some point your Leadership team will be looking around for who can fill the next Leadership role.

HINT: If you start educating yourself and demonstrating Leadership NOW, you can avoid the "first supervisor blues."

The "blues" are that set of emotions and circumstances that face the first-time supervisor or team Leader.

You will probably find your first Leadership role to be the "lead worker" or equivalent in the group you are in right now.

In that role, you'll find out if your team respects you and sees you as decisive and competent. You can prepare yourself for that first time you have to correct a "friend."

During one role in my career, I researched complaints and other issues related to supervisor – employee relationships.

We discovered that half of all complaints about supervisor behavior involved first-time Leaders.

Perhaps even more telling was that 35 additional percentage of complaints were related to repeat "offenders."

Take an honest look at your Leadership. How often have you said something that you never followed up on? In the early days, you may have had the full intention of acting.

Looking back, you might now realize that you "overpromised" because you wanted to be appreciated, at least for the "effort."

And then you get away with not doing what you promised by blaming budgets or higher-ups or some unknown circumstance.

No one criticizes you (you think). Then it happens again.

Do you see how this could develop into a pattern?

Eventually you convince yourself that your team just needs emotional propping up. Before long, self-deception leads you to believe that what really matters is to "talk a good game" as if nobody remembers your broken promises.

But they do.

The next time you address your team, formally or informally, plan what you are going to say. Don't promise what you can't or won't deliver. Tell the truth. It works every time it's tried! Your team will appreciate the candor.

#10

"Evaluations Aren't Important"

"I don't have time to keep up with everyone's actual performance, so I give everyone the same evaluation."

It's a lie.

We've repeated the theme throughout this book. It is your job to LEAD your team. That includes taking the time to keep a confidential performance file on your team members.

How can your team operate at peak performance if you aren't working to help them improve?

I've invented a scientific explanation for those who believe this lie. The word for it comes from an ancient Greek term describing a lack of full brain function, *'Laye-see'*.

It means just what you think it means, lazy! There really is no other excuse.

In one large state agency, one of my responsibilities was to review the employee evaluations submitted by supervisors and managers.

Each employee was to be rated from One to Five. Employees with a "One" would likely be in line to be fired.

Employees with a "Five" were considered the very highest-level performers. The policy at the time was to award pay raises in proportion to the rating.

A rating of three (meets expectations) would get a basic pay raise, a four (exceeds expectations) would get a bit more pay raise and a five (far exceeds expectations) would get the highest possible pay raise.

> *"Employees who report receiving recognition and praise within the last seven days show increased productivity, get higher scores from customers, and have better safety records. They're just more engaged at work."*
>
> *– Tom Rath*

The rule of thumb was that the budget probably only provided for about 20% of the employees to be given raises above the basic rate.

One particular manager took this budgetary estimate quite literally.

His annual evaluations for 80% of his employees were brief and to the point: "Employee meets expectations for this requirement, Rating is 3."

This would be listed for every section of their job duties and therefore the employee would get an overall rating of "3."

For the other 20% of the team, allegedly chosen randomly, the evaluations read: "Employee exceeds expectations for this requirement, Rating is 4."

The overall rating then was also a "4."

No employees were rated at a "5."

So, I asked the manager why every single evaluation was like this.

His honest but simplistic explanation astounded me.

This manager stated that he knew that giving a "5" required additional documentation and he didn't have any. Therefore, he gave no employee that rating, whether they may have deserved it or not.

He explained further, "I wanted to give extra pay raises to the office staff, so I rated 20% at "exceeds expectations" and figured I'd rotate another group to a "4" next year so they would get the extra pay raise. In a few years everybody would get the extra money."

The fact was that, with proper documentation, more employees could have the higher pay raise percentage than he had reported! His effort to "give a bigger pay raise" may have actually deprived some employees of the pay raise they had earned.

Believing this lie had led this manager to a misguided - even if well-meaning pathway.

But he had that "Laye-see" disease and had not taken the time to monitor and properly evaluate the work of his staff.

I had a recent conversation with an upper level manager who had a promising first level supervisor who asked to be relieved of their duties. The request was based on a lack of support from his area manager to correct the poor performance of an employee.

The poor employee performance was having a contagious effect on other employees and desperately needed to be addressed.

The upper level manager appealed to the new supervisor to keep the job and properly document the poor performance and promised full support for any action that might need to be taken to correct the behavior or remove the employee.

But there was no promise from the mid-manager who had failed to support the supervisor initially.

The sad ending to this story is that the new supervisor stuck with her request to take a voluntary demotion from the job.

Failing to provide as well as support accurately documented evaluations and not only affects the individual employee involved but discourages your subordinate Leaders. In this case a good Leader was lost and time will have to be spent finding a replacement.

The costs of believing this lie are enormous.

Ultimately, properly documented employee performance rewards the deserving and can remove troublesome individuals.

We too often forget the "bad apple" analogy. Corrected or removing "infectious" poor performers can improve the performance of the rest of your team. Don't underestimate the power of influence!

Failing to do so can have disastrous unintended consequences.

Believing this lie also deprives you of one of the best management tools in your toolbox – Accountability!

By failing to hold team members accountable, you perpetuate a "Whatever" mentality as we discussed in the "Socializing" chapter.

It is extremely difficult to lead a team with a "whatever" attitude. As with the tool of Inspiration, the Tool of Accountability can change a "whatever" to a "whatever it takes."

The fact is that though most employees desire some flexibility in their own work patterns, they also yearn for consistency, structure and discipline.

When you discount performance appraisals and regular feedback, you forfeit a powerful management and Leadership tool.

#11

"I'm Indispensable!"

Or put another way, "This place would fall apart without me."

This lie is based on a similar selfdeception as some of these other lies: I am smart, important and I can do whatever I want.

Sometimes this lie reflects a self-fulfilling prophecy. That is, you haven't led or managed well enough to be sure that no one is indispensable, including yourself.

> *"Don't think of yourself as indispensable or infallible. As Charles De Gaulle said, 'the cemeteries of the world are full of indispensable men.'"*
>
> *- Donald Rumsfeld*

That false narrative begins with a lack of trust of your team members, as we discussed before.

Leaders who aren't personally secure or professionally secure, tend to circle the wagons, trust no one and look out for themselves only.

In one organization, a reorganization was in the works. Two work units were about to be consolidated.

A meeting of the managers of both groups was scheduled to make the announcement of who would become the head of the new, consolidated work group.

In the larger of the two groups, the senior-most manager gathered all his subordinate managers in his office just prior to the announcement meeting.

This Leader directed his managers to march into the meeting behind him like a band following the Drum Major.

It was clear he wished to show that his managers were in solidarity behind his "indispensable" Leadership.

To his disappointment, the senior-most manager of the *smaller* group was appointed to head the consolidated group instead.

The "Drum Major" Leader, who had led the largest group in the entire organization was relegated to a relatively minor role until his retirement. He became, in political terms, a lame duck.

Building a "kingdom" centered on yourself is creating a structure with a weak foundation. The larger the organization becomes, the more likely the foundation will crumble and bring the organization down with it.

If you have believed that you are indispensable, you need to face the harsh reality that *no one* is indispensable.

Perhaps you have too closely connected your personal self-worth with work. That is a foundation built on shifting sand and will wash away as surely as the next wave that hits the beach.

You cannot always be "in control." In fact, you *aren't* in control now, you have just convinced yourself that you are!

If you are always being asked to do something because you are "available" or "you always do it," perhaps you are not indispensable, you are being taken advantage of!

There is a difference between being valuable and being indispensable.

When you feel indispensable, you set yourself up to being "used."

No matter what your role in your organization, you *can* and you *will* be replaced. Whether voluntarily or by force, the day will come when your time is done.

Playing the "I'm Indispensable" card is a losing hand.

#12

"It's Better To Not Make Hard Decisions"

The corollary to this lie is that, "Making controversial decisions is the way I get in trouble."

Sometimes this lie takes the form of, "Don't rock the boat," or "If I just give them enough space, their behavior or work performance will improve."

No matter how you say it, this lie will sabotage your work place or organization.

The scientific theory called, "The Second Law of Thermodynamics" applies here. Don't worry, this writer is certainly no science geek so here it is in plain English.

> *"Shelving hard decisions is the least ethical course."*
>
> *- Adrian Cadbury*

If you leave an object (or an organization) without intervention, it will decline or decay to a worse condition over time.

Throughout this book, we have emphasized that the job of the Leader is to Lead! It sounds so obvious but that is part of the problem. We often overlook the truths that are right in front of our eyes.

"Dan" was a customer service rep in one organization, who was continually the subject of complaints from their customers.

His immediate manager did his best to ignore or minimize the complaints and was motivated to insulate the problem from the next higher-level manager.

The upper level manager had created a culture of non-intervention. The first level manager was simply following the example set for him.

This non-interventional approach had multiple negative results.

First, the employee's work performance did not and would not improve. This culture deprived the employee of the needed coaching needed to improve his work.

The lack of work improvement hurt the organization's reputation in the community.

The other employees labeled the management as weak and indifferent. That resulted in a lack of motivation to excel and a lower level of product quality and quantity.

Over time, this particular upper level manager gained a negative reputation with the highest-level Leaders in the organization.

Later this manager applied for a higher-level Leadership position in the organization.

The hiring Leader asked for my help in politely but properly wording the reasons why his selection was someone other than the manager above.

I asked, "Well, exactly what was your thinking?"

His answer was eye-opening to say the least.

"I didn't pick [the manager above] because I think I would always have to spend time telling him what to do. With the one I selected, I might have to reign him in, but that would be less time consuming."

Failure to lead your organization will stifle your own career. Don't let that happen!

So then, why do Leaders believe this lie that it's better to not make hard decisions, when the consequences are so broad?

Simply put, believing this lie is usually based on fear – fear of the consequences of poor decisions.

Leadership is not for the faint of heart. It can be difficult and even painful, but the rewards are inversely satisfying and rewarding.

Trust me – you will make mistakes. You will make wrong decisions and choices.

Overcoming the often paralyzing effects of this fear is a key factor in whether you will succeed or fail as a Leader.

Believing this lie and refusing to make real decisions also shows a failure to look far enough into the future.

Every step – or failure to take a step – can cripple an organization. Avoiding decisions is avoiding the future.

> *"You've got to know when to hold 'em, know when to fold 'em, know when to walk away, know when to run."*
>
> *- Kenny Rogers*

Great Leaders are ahead of the curve in the life cycle of an organization. The Leader's job is all about tomorrow and the day after.

You can't afford to look the other way. Problems will not go away on their own.

It's been said that the speed with which you overcome challenges ultimately determines you long term success as a Leader.

Don't cheat yourself out of the positive effects of knowing that you've made a contribution to your organization and the world around you!

#13

"Whatever Happened Before Isn't Important"

Some Leaders believe the lie that the culture and history of an organization isn't important.

"After all, I'm in charge now," they seem to say.

We're certainly not the first to quote the old axiom that those who don't learn from the past are doomed to repeat it.

It's become such a part of the modern lexicon that we gloss over any thought of it.

> *"Culture eats strategy for breakfast."*
>
> *-Peter Drucker*

DON'T!

Failing to navigate the shark infested waters of corporate culture will doom your future as a Leader.

Take for example the case of the Leader Larry who was selected to be the manager of a work unit in a small town far from the company headquarters. As it turned out, the CEO maintained a home near that town. Traditionally, the CEO would drive "home" on weekends and often stop by that office.

Tradition had also dictated that this location would designate office space for the CEO "just in case" it was needed.

When the new manager was selected, he was called to his immediate Leader's office before taking the role in the new town.

Leader Larry was cautioned about making changes too quickly. In fact, he was directed to not make any major changes at all for one full year.

So he maintained the CEO's mostly empty office at the expense of his own work unit's space needs. He maintained the status quo against his nature and temperament and often complained in private to fellow managers about his "handcuffs" as he put it.

After that first year, he began to implement various improvements in office procedures and work assignments.

By this time the CEO had moved on. But the employees he "inherited" complained loud and long simply because changes were made.

When those complaints reached upper management, it was clear the only objections were unfounded.

The patient understanding of the culture had won Leader Larry the favor of upper management.

Contrast this Leader with Manager Mary.

Manager Mary had supervised a work unit for several years and was promoted to manage a unit with a very different set of responsibilities.

Mary immediately modified several process and procedures including the requirement that certain decisions could only be made by her.

Some directives were given that not only slowed certain processes but did not follow required legal protocol.

Mary's failure to consult with long term subordinates regarding processes and legal requirements caused her new team to doubt her ability and wisdom.

> *"He who thinks he leads, but has no followers, is only taking a walk."*
>
> *- John Maxwell*

Mary reacted to the resistance as if it were insubordination. Do I need to tell you that Manager Mary's career came to a screeching halt?

When budgetary stress called for cost cutting measures, Mary was first in line to go.

Her disruptive methods demonstrated a lack of understanding of her team's mission and a seeming disregard for her team members.

She failed to understand the culture of her new work unit and it cost her.

But it's also important to look at culture on a more personal level.

Whether you are in a position of Leadership or considered a journeyman employee, your work patterns were probably influenced by another employee. This is often true even if there was a formal training program in which you participated.

So-called "model employees" will pass along their own attitudes and habits – for better or worse.

As a result, most Leaders treat others the way they were treated. You are bound to find gaps in your preparation that show up in crisis situations just like Manager Mary.

Even before you are selected for Leadership, take time to reflect on the ways you were led.

- What tactics positively motivated you?
- What did not work?
- Were you shown an example leading toward continuous personal improvement?
- What are the dominant attitudes of the organization or work unit?
- Is there a reputation for high quality work?

These influences can be subtle, but they are real. Take personal responsibility for your own work patterns as well as your knowledge base.

When you take on a new Leadership role, find out about the culture. Is usage of leave time frowned upon? Is your team expected to work extra hours when needed?

Then, work to form win-win relationships with other Leaders. Find common ground with your new team and look to understand their motivations. Share your goals and vision in a way that garners support.

When employees believe you "understand" them, they are much more likely to buy-in to your plans. Take the time it will require to build their trust.

It will be worth it.

#14

"It's Not My Fault"

Have you heard yourself saying these words? It's another one of those true-isms that we never assign to ourselves, right?

We quickly identify politicians as being the individuals who notoriously refuse to be accountable for their mistakes, but business and community Leaders are guilty too.

Even if only few people are aware of the mistake, declining to accept responsibility will seriously damage a Leader's credibility and reputation. Being a Leader requires a high level of confidence to say, "the buck stops here."

Admittedly, we live in a lawsuit-silly society. We have learned to deflect blame and accuse someone else of wrong-doing which brought negative results.

Rather, a great Leader tends to accept the blame, even when it does not entirely rest on her shoulders.

Former Navy Commander Scott Waddle was Captain of the US nuclear submarine, USS

> *"Let us be thankful for fools. But for them, the rest of us would not succeed."*
>
> *- Mark Twain*

Greenville. In February 2001, the sub collided with a Japanese fishing boat, resulting in nine deaths.

Unlike many other Leaders in the public eye who have denied or made excuses for their behavior, Commander Waddle stood boldly and took complete responsibility for his actions. It's a lesson we all can learn from.

Too often, when things go well and the team succeeds, the Leader is quick to "swoop in" and take the credit. Or, when things fail, they are quick to put the blame on someone else.

You've heard the ways sports coaches deflect blame and put it on their team:

- "Mistakes killed us," (my players blew it).

- "The best team won," (our players aren't that good).
- "We got outplayed," (I didn't play badly, the team did).

When you blame others, you prevent yourself from being able to do proper self-evaluation, which is critical to self-improvement.

Real Leaders step aside and make sure every team member feels appreciated for their contribution to the team.

The Leader who doesn't blame others has his office in the *solutions department*, not the *excuses department*.

When you take responsibility for mistakes, even when your direct involvement may have been cursory, you win the trust and appreciation of your team.

#15

"I Have to Watch Everyone"

Some Leaders have found themselves believing the lie that they have to be in the middle of everything.

The usual mis-belief is based on a combination of "I'm Indispensable," "I'm The Leader Because I'm Smarter," and "People Are the Problem."

It's Micromanaging. Pure and simple.

In my experience and based on interviews with dozens of Leaders, micromanagers generally do not believe they are micromanaging.

That's part of the problem. Micromanagers seem to have a need for control which stems from their anxious Leadership tendencies.

Here are some of the warning signs and questions for you to ask yourself:

- Do you get involved with the work of others without speaking to them first?
- Do you find yourself looking at details rather than the big picture?
- Do you tend to discourage others from making decisions?

- Are the reports you require asking for relatively unimportant details?
- Do you find yourself believing you have no one to whom you can delegate work?
- Does your team seem to be unmotivated?
- Do you privately believe that if you want something done right, you must do it yourself?

Clearly there are other characteristics, but these questions are a good start in some self-evaluation.

Micromanagement is nothing more than bad management.

Among the net results for a micromanager is a loss of trust. Your team will begin to see you as a dictator, not a Leader.

Much like other "lies" we've discussed, micromanaging will cause your team to withdraw from making reasonable decisions for fear that you will overturn them.

> *"Never tell people how to do things. Tell them what to do and they will surprise you with their ingenuity."*
>
> *– General George Patton*

They will think, "No matter what I do, it won't be good enough."

By micromanaging, you discount the skills, ability and experience of your team members.

They will figure that out and stop fighting

for input. The ultimate result is your own failure and burnout.

I believe that micromanagers do not intend to do harm. But, there is no real difference between unintentional harm and intentional harm.

One recently appointed Micromanager was overheard discussing the details of an upcoming conference scheduled. Rather than ask about the invitation list or the program, this Micromanager berated an employee over the *size of the cookies* to be served!

If you are a micromanager, try these tips to make some reasonable changes in your management techniques:

- Make an honest assessment of your behavior.

- Begin to delegate reasonable tasks to trustworthy employees.
- Build your trust profile by gradually increasing the significance of delegated tasks.
- Have regular meetings with those doing delegated work but keep them very short – ask for just an overview.

If you work for a micromanager, try these steps to mitigate the effects.

- Be sure that you are giving your work your full attention.
- Be honest and discover if you have given your manager any reason to mistrust you.

- Find out what is most important to your micromanager.
- Meet frequently (and usually briefly if possible).

Micromanaging is always a lose-lose proposition. Fight the urge to control every aspect of your team's work.

You will be pleasantly surprised at the results and your own well-being.

Don't get caught in the micromanaging trap!

#16

"That's Not Important"

In contrast to the micro-manager, some Leaders swing the pendulum too far in the other direction. Somewhat related to the Leader who believes the lie that a "make no decision" point of view, this Leader simply delegates so much that her team members believe she is out of touch.

This is the MACRO-manager.

This Leader walks a tightrope between delegation and disconnection.

It's not that this Leader can't or won't delegate, but that perhaps it has been done unwisely.

I worked in one organization where the Chief Executive Officer of the work unit was a delegator. He had given great latitude to the Deputy who carried out those duties efficiently and properly.

In fact, the Deputy had a great track record of Leadership and had earned the trust of the CEO.

The Deputy routinely made decisions without consulting the CEO. The Deputy had learned which decisions needed to be approved by the CEO in advance and which ones he should tell the CEO afterward.

The Deputy met regularly with the CEO and they maintained quite a very good working relationship.

The issue that arose was that the organization's lower level managers and team members began to think the Deputy was the primary decision-maker.

This is the fear many Leaders face and hinders delegation.

The reputation of the CEO developed that he was aloof and

> *Surround yourself with the best people you can find, delegate authority, and don't interfere as long as the policy you've decided upon is being carried out.*
>
> *- Ronald Reagan*

disconnected from the work unit. This was not the case at all.

However, the perception of who he was didn't wane. There were several steps that needed to have been taken to prevent that misconception.

First, the CEO had a propensity to work in or close to his office on projects few knew about. It would have been helpful for the CEO to have ventured beyond the corner office more frequently.

In fact, with the CEO's ability to delegate, he could have redirected his schedule to spend more time with rank and file employees.

Also, the Deputy could have and should have clarified to his direct reports that ultimate decisions rested with the CEO. Privately, the Deputy had, instead, spoken of ways to get around the CEO's objections to certain initiatives.

However, both the CEO and the Deputy had become comfortable with the arrangement. The CEO was never fully aware that his subordinates thought of him as "uninvolved."

The Deputy was later promoted to a CEO role in another work unit.

Delegation is an important skill for Leaders. It must be carried out with careful skill and a full awareness of the consequences. In circumstances as we have described above, is it any wonder that insecure Leaders choose not to delegate.

The so-called "SMART" system of delegation is a good model to follow.

However, let me make one modification to the acronym and make it the **"SMARTR"** system.

That is, delegation should be:

- **S**pecific – be specific in your project assignments rather than open ended
- **M**easurable – have a detailed, data driven method for evaluating the delegated task
- **A**chievable – make sure your subordinates have the skills and tools to accomplish the task
- **R**elevant – make the assignment is related to the customary work of the team member
- **T**ime-Sensitive – be sure a reasonable deadline has been agreed upon, and

- **Relational** – be sure to connect with the team member and others about the project being delegated.

This last addition to the acronym will give "authority" to the team member to whom you have delegated the project yet clarify that you are still ultimately responsible.

If you follow the **SMARTR** system, you'll find delegation will be easier for you if you've been resistant.

If you already delegate, this additional step will help prevent the impression that you believe the "That's Not Important" lie.

Epilogue

It would be hard to imagine that any of us have not drifted toward these lies and myths at some point or another. To have experienced that simply would mean that we have a birth certificate – we are human!

You might be asking, "So, how do I break the pattern of the lie or lies I've been believing (and living)?"

Admittedly, it takes some self-reflection. But a good start is simply admitting that a destructive pattern exists. This may be the most difficult step – it is certainly the most important!

First, get tough on yourself. Give your self-discipline a boost. You can do that by:

- Define or refine your core personal values. Decide who you really are.
- In a new project, break it down into small steps.
- Respect your time and the time of others.

- Take time to decide how you would want to be treated when dealing with other people.
- Prioritize steps of a project to reach your goal as efficiently as possible.
- Visualize the end result and anticipate the satisfaction that will come.

Then, give yourself permission to change – and permission to get back up when you stumble back into the "Lie" behavior. Refusing to allow yourself to change can become a fatal error.

Begin to associate yourself with those whom you know are leading well. There may be some lies they are still believing but learn from their better behaviors.

You can choose your attitude. Choose an optimistic, positive one every day.

A good attitude will help you overcome adversity. A Poor attitude will cause adversity to overcome you.

Let your positive attitude be seen by the highest and lowest you come into contact with. Your attitude can open doors and shape other people's lives!

Measure your progress by an objective standard. We tend to shortchange our progress when we only compare our progress to how we "used to be." To say, "Well, at least I'm not like I was," or "I'm not as bad as 'Joe'," is giving yourself permission to fail.

Finally, keep looking to improve. Becoming a great Leader is a lifelong project.

Pass along nuggets of experience. Model great Leadership to those you can influence.

Whether your "work" career is just beginning or nearing its end, you will find yourself leading in many ways for the rest of your life – do it well!

Selected Resources

"Amplified Leadership," - Dan Reiland

"Intentional Living," - John Maxwell

"The 17 Indisputable Laws of Teamwork
    – John Maxwell

"Rules & Tools for Leaders" – Gen. Perry Smith

"Managing Your Manager," Gonzague Dufour

"The Absolutes of Leadership," – Philip Crosby

"Rumsfeld's Rules" – Donald Rumsfeld

"Be the Leader You Were Meant to Be,"
    - Leroy Eims

"The 10 Natural Laws of Successful Time and Life Management," – Hyrum Smith

www.ingramcontent.com/pod-product-compliance
Lightning Source LLC
Chambersburg PA
CBHW021819170526
45157CB00007B/2644